Until one day a spacecraft zooms by.
Closer. And closer.

Its long legs reach down.
Finally it touches the ground.

A man carefully places his boot on the gray dust.
"That's one small step for man," he says, "one giant leap
for mankind."

The moon's first visitor, Neil Armstrong, has arrived!

Soon Buzz Aldrin joins him. The two bounce across the surface in a jog-hop moon walk. Even with heavy backpacks, the astronauts weigh much less than they do on Earth, thanks to the moon's lower gravity.

Not a minute to waste! They gather rocks, snap pictures, and proudly plant an American flag.

A silvery dot disappears into the blackness.
Silence, again.

9

# APOLLO 12
## NOVEMBER 19–20, 1969

Four months later another ship appears.

    The pilot, Pete Conrad, scours the shadowy surface for his target: a group of craters that looks like a huge snowman.

    His goal is to land inside the snowman's belly button.

    The ship zigs right.

    It zags left.

Then it lands with a thump—right on target.

"Good landing, Pete!" crewmate Alan Bean says.

Back on Earth, mission control cheers. This precise landing means future astronauts can choose where they'll explore.

Eager to uncover the moon's many secrets, Alan hammers
a tube into the ground to collect soil.

Pete sets up an experiment to measure the sun's energy.

The explorers collect rocks and take pictures.

But much too soon they must head for home.

# APOLLO 13
## APRIL 15, 1970

The moon patiently waits several months.

    Then one day a spacecraft zooms over its far side.
But the ship doesn't slow down. It doesn't land.

    It just speeds by, with three brave astronauts shivering inside.
They look longingly at the moon below—the marvelous place
they'd dreamed of exploring.

    But that dream ended yesterday, when an explosion shook
their craft, and their confidence.

Now they're running out of power, oxygen, and hope.
They must return to Earth as fast as they can.
The moon lends a helping hand. Its gravity pulls the
injured spaceship faster and faster, then slings it toward home.

Once on the moon, Alan spies a brilliant blue jewel in
the black sky—Earth. Tears of joy fill his eyes.
Then he looks down at the long list of jobs on his sleeve.
Time to get to work.

When his tasks are done, Alan pulls out two golf balls he
smuggled aboard.

Millions of people back home watch as he swings his
homemade club. *Smack!* Alan becomes the first golfer in space!

# APOLLO 15
## JULY 30–AUGUST 2, 1971

All alone the moon circles Earth—174 more days. Then a ship named Falcon swoops in. Dave Scott and Jim Irwin have come to explore the moon's mighty mountains. And they've brought something new: a lunar rover!

Seat belts fastened tight, the two speed over the dusty land. Dave drives the rover as fast as it will go, so they'll have more time to explore. Every time they hit a rock, the rover soars through the air.

Dave and Jim park the rover and hike up a steep mountain. Their boots sink into the loose dust. The climb is exhausting, yet they don't give up.

Their goal is to find a white rock called anorthosite. This ancient rock was part of the moon's original crust.

They discover gray rocks, green rocks—even rocks with bits of glass.

But no anorthosite.

The next day they use a rake to uncover rocks beneath
the dust.

Still no luck.

Then Dave spies something white in the distance.
Could it be? He moves closer and brushes off some
moondust. The rock sparkles in the sun.

"I think we found what we came for!" Dave exclaims.

# Apollo 16
## April 21–24, 1972

Eight months later the moon welcomes John Young and Charlie Duke.

They can't wait to explore an area no one has visited: the moon's highlands.

Scientists think the craters there were formed by erupting volcanoes. To prove this, the astronauts must find rocks made of lava.

As the rover heads for the highlands, its tires slide over the fine moondust. "It's just like driving on snow!" John says.

The men hunt and hunt for lava rocks, but find something surprising instead: rocks created long ago by meteors crashing into the moon.

Their discovery means the craters were made by meteors, not volcanoes.

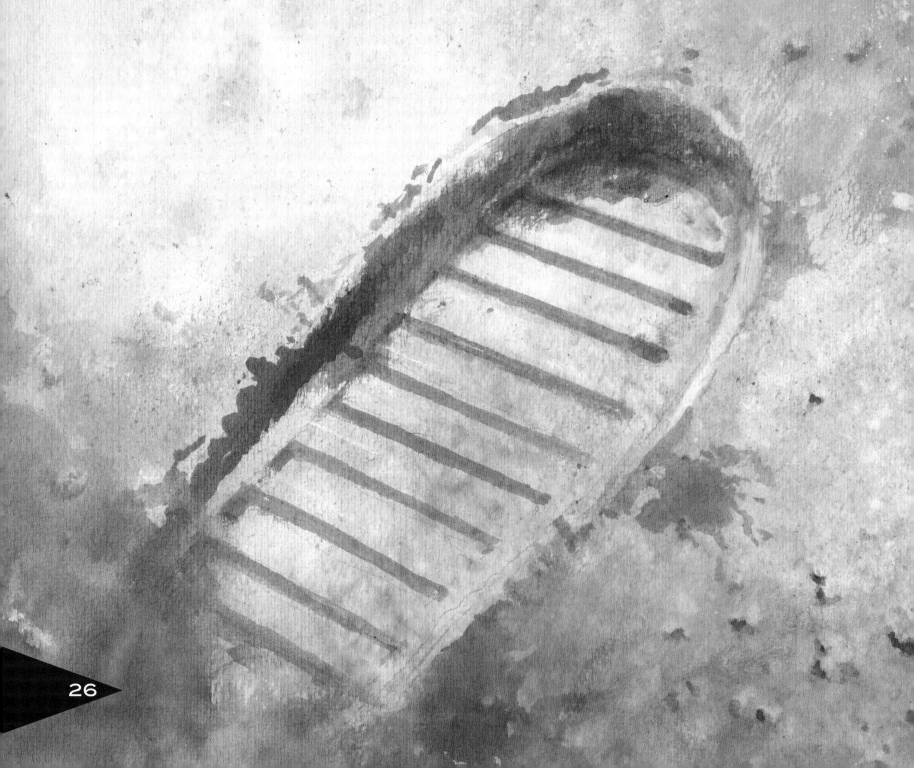

The astronauts collect many treasures during their visit.
On the last day Charlie gives the moon one of his greatest
treasures: a picture of his family.

# APOLLO 17
## DECEMBER 11–14, 1972

Before long, two more space voyagers arrive. Gene Cernan and Jack Schmitt have brought enough supplies to stay more than three days—the longest visit yet.

The explorers discover orange soil, precious titanium metal, and a boulder as big as a house. On their last day Gene finds an unusual rock made of many small, different-colored rocks. It reminds him of the many people who make up his home—Earth.

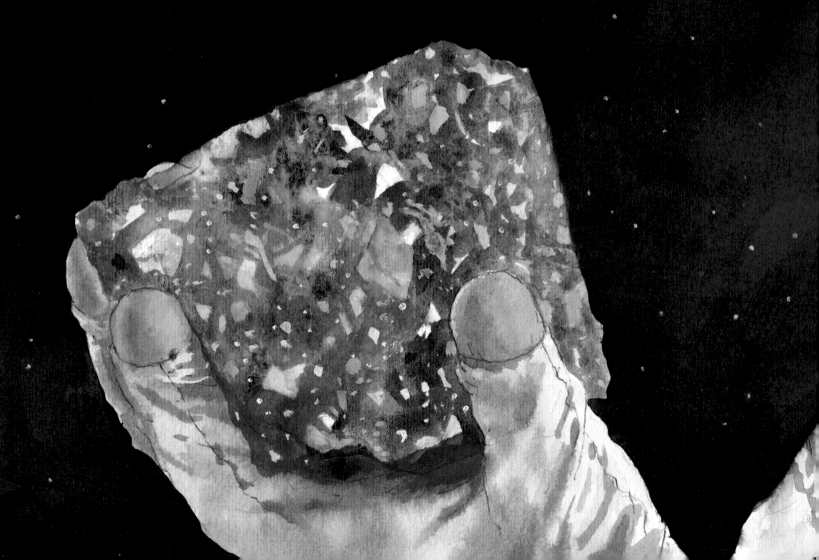

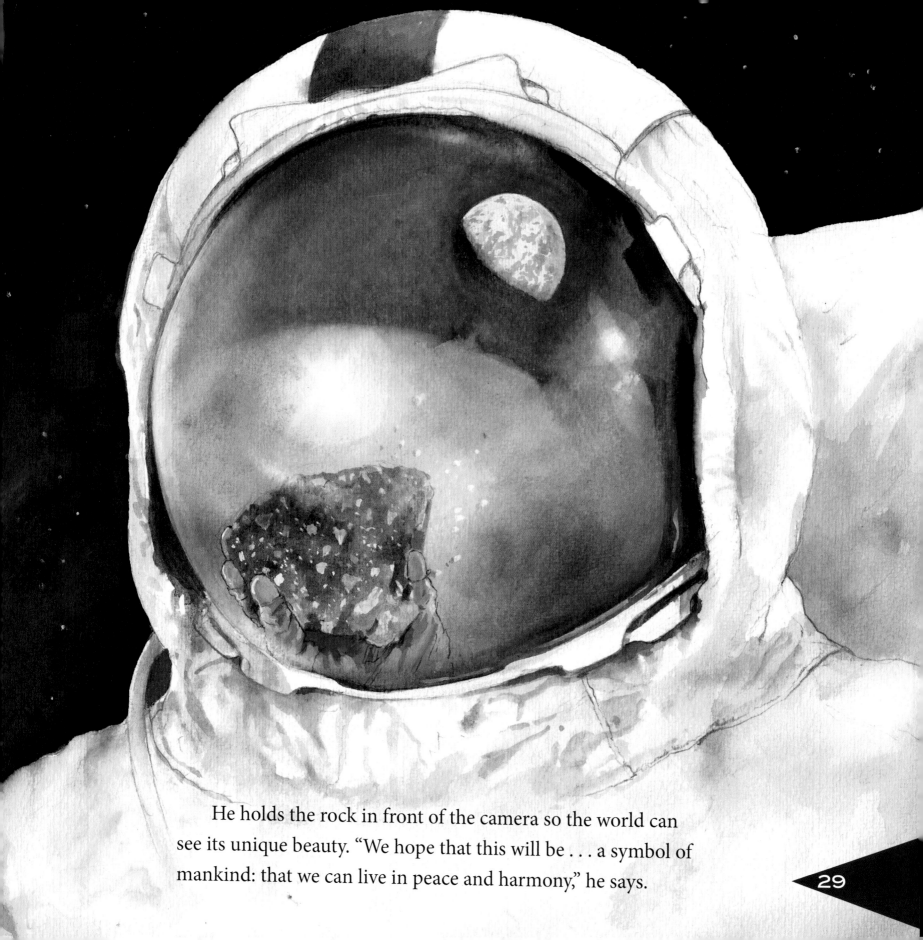

He holds the rock in front of the camera so the world can see its unique beauty. "We hope that this will be . . . a symbol of mankind: that we can live in peace and harmony," he says.

Gene climbs onto the ladder one last time,
leaving the last footprint on the moon for decades—
maybe forever.

A sleepy engine wakes.
A tiny ship rises and soars through the black sea of space.
Home.

# Afterword
## Alan Bean, Fourth Man on the Moon

I'm often asked, "When you first stepped on the moon, what were your thoughts?" Although that moment was the culmination of many dreams and fears, successes and failures—none of that was on my mind. Instead, I was thinking I had to learn how to move in one-sixth gravity as fast as I could. Only then would I be able to do the tasks on the checklist strapped to my wrist, such as gather rocks and set up experiments.

It didn't take long to learn how to run in a space suit. The knee and hip joints were stiff, but the ankle joints moved easily. So I kept my legs relatively stiff and mostly used ankle motions. It felt and looked as if I were dancing on tiptoe. On Earth I weighed about three hundred pounds with my suit and backpack. On the moon my equipment and I weighed only fifty pounds. This light weight made me feel super strong, as if I could run forever.

"This is the moon," I said in disbelief to my crewmate Pete Conrad while looking down at the dusty gray surface. Then I squinted and stared up at that beautiful crescent Earth and said, "That is the Earth!" It was hard to believe we were standing on our only moon.

# A Note from the Author

I am greatly indebted to astronaut Alan Bean (1932–2018) for his email correspondence and telephone interviews, and for graciously answering many questions and sharing fascinating details about his moon mission. I am also grateful to Joel Kowsky, photo editor and photographer at NASA, for his assistance. Also, my thanks to Roger Papet, Fred Grant, and Roy Lovejoy, my engineering coworkers at McDonnell Douglas Space Systems, who many years ago welcomed me to the team and generously shared their expertise.

# Time Line to the Moon

1958: NASA (National Aeronautics and Space Administration) is founded.

1961: Alan Shepard pilots the Mercury spacecraft Freedom 7 and becomes the first American in space (May 5).

1965–66: Project Gemini flies ten missions in low Earth orbit to prepare for the Apollo moon missions.

1968: The first manned Apollo mission, Apollo 7, lifts off on October 11 and tests a command module in Earth orbit.

1968: Apollo 8 launches on December 21 and orbits the moon ten times.

1969: Apollo 9 launches on March 3 and tests a lunar module in Earth orbit.

1969: Apollo 10 launches on May 18 and flies within 9 miles (14 kilometers) of the moon.

1969: Apollo 11 astronaut Neil Armstrong becomes the first human on the moon (July 20).

1969: Apollo 12 makes a precise moon landing November 19 and conducts extensive tests on the moon.

1970: Apollo 13 launches on April 11, but the astronauts are not able to land on the moon due to an oxygen tank explosion.

1971: Apollo 14 arrives February 5 on the lunar highlands.

1971: Apollo 15 lands July 30 with a lunar rover, which allows further moon exploration.

1972: Apollo 16 crew arrives April 21 and explores the central highlands.

1972: Apollo 17 astronauts land December 11 and conduct the longest, most extensive lunar explorations.

Present: More lunar missions are being planned. Someday, women and men from all over the world may walk on the moon. Maybe you will, too!

# More About the Vehicles

The daring dozen trained many years for their moon expeditions, but these missions would not have been possible without the dedication of a diverse team of more than four hundred thousand men and women. This team included mathematicians, computer programmers, machinists, engineers, assembly workers, suit designers, geologists, and more.

Together the team created extraordinary vehicles that carried the crew 240,000 miles (386,000 kilometers) to the moon, allowed them to explore the lunar surface, and returned them safely home.

**Saturn V** (five): The powerful rocket that launched each Apollo moon mission. Standing 363 feet (111 meters) tall, this rocket was made of three large pieces, or "stages." Each stage ignited at a different time to push the rocket on its path to the moon. The first stage lifted the Apollo spacecraft off the launchpad and carried it to an altitude of about 42 miles (68 kilometers) before disconnecting from the rocket and dropping into the ocean. Then the second stage fired and pushed the spacecraft higher into space before also falling into the ocean. Finally the third stage ignited and continued pushing the spacecraft on its journey to the moon.

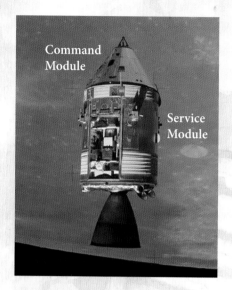

Command Module

Service Module

**Command Module (CM):** The gumdrop-shaped capsule on top of the rocket. Three astronauts rode inside the CM to and from the moon. Once the CM entered lunar orbit, it circled the moon until it was time to return home. After reentering Earth's atmosphere, the CM splashed down into the ocean.

**Service Module (SM):** The large metal cylinder attached to the CM. The SM held supplies such as oxygen and electricity. It also had a small engine to move it into and out of lunar orbit.

**Lunar Module (LM):** The bug-like craft that carried two astronauts from the orbiting CM to the surface of the moon and back. (The third astronaut, the command module pilot, remained in the CM.) The LM served as a temporary home for the astronauts during their stay on the moon.

**Lunar Roving Vehicle (LRV):** The battery-powered car used by Apollo 15, 16, and 17. On flat ground the rover's top speed was 8 miles per hour (13 kilometers per hour). This may not seem fast, but it saved the crew precious energy on long workdays. Wire mesh around the rover's metal wheels provided traction on loose, fine moondust. Astronauts used a control stick to steer, accelerate, or stop the vehicle. The rover's umbrella-like TV antenna sent live video to Earth. Its radio antenna allowed astronauts to talk to mission control.

# More About the Moon Missions

The main goal of the first moon mission, Apollo 11, was to land on the moon and bring the astronauts safely home. Future missions spent more time on the moon and explored larger areas. Every lunar module landed in a new location so its crew could explore different geographic features. Moon landings were planned so the crew arrived during the lunar day, when the sun was shining.

Each Apollo flight built on the successes of earlier missions, yet every launch, spaceflight, landing, and moon walk was extremely dangerous. One small mistake or one tiny equipment failure could mean disaster. Amazingly, six of the seven Apollo moon missions successfully landed and returned home. Though an explosion scrubbed Apollo 13's landing, the dedicated ground crew devised a plan to bring the astronauts back alive.

To this day, the Apollo program remains one of the most incredible achievements in history.

# More About the Art

Apollo astronauts wore helmets equipped with visors to protect their eyes from the bright sun. The astronauts could slide the visors up and down as needed. In some illustrations, you can see the astronaut's face through the clear protective visor. In other illustrations, the gold-colored sun visor is down, so all you see is its reflective finish.

You might have noticed that some astronaut suits have red stripes, while others don't. The Apollo 11 and 12 astronauts wore identical suits, which made it difficult to identify individuals in photographs. To solve this problem, the commander's suit and helmet had red stripes from Apollo 13 on.

The illustrations of the moon's sky show what's actually there: stars sparkling in black space. Yet photos from the moon don't show stars, because cameras must use a very fast shutter speed to capture images on such a bright surface. A short exposure time can't capture light from tiny stars. Bright sunlight and protective visors prevented the astronauts from viewing stars—although some spotted a few bright stars while standing in the lunar module's shadow.

# Apollo 11

Commander: Neil Armstrong (left)

Command module pilot: Michael Collins (center)

Lunar module pilot: Edwin "Buzz" Aldrin Jr. (right)

Launch: July 16, 1969

Moon landing: July 20, 1969

Splashdown: July 24, 1969

Command module: Columbia

Lunar module: Eagle

Total time on moon: 21 hours, 38 minutes

Surface EVAs*: 1

EVA time: 2 hours, 31 minutes

*EVA (Extravehicular Activity): Astronaut exploration outside the spacecraft.
Slightly different EVA times appear in different sources. The times in this book are
from the Smithsonian National Air and Space Museum website (see page 47).

*Buzz Aldrin admires the first flag on the moon.
A rod in the top of the flag made it look like it
was flying.*

During Apollo 11's short stay on the moon, the astronauts had many important jobs to do. Surprisingly, Buzz Aldrin worried most about planting the flag. With millions of people watching on live TV, he wanted the historic event to go smoothly. The astronauts pushed down on the aluminum pole as hard as they could, but it went only a few inches into the rocky soil. Much to Buzz's relief, it stayed upright. Apollo 11 carried home the first samples of rocks and soil from the moon. Scientists were fascinated to discover that the moon's maria (the dark sections that look like oceans) are made of basalt, a common volcanic rock on Earth. The moon samples also proved what scientists had believed for years: that there's no life on the moon.

# APOLLO 12

Commander: Charles "Pete" Conrad Jr. (left)

Command module pilot: Richard "Dick" Gordon Jr. (center)

Lunar module pilot: Alan Bean (right)

Launch: November 14, 1969

Moon landing: November 19, 1969

Splashdown: November 24, 1969

Command module: Yankee Clipper

Lunar module: Intrepid

Total time on moon: 31 hours, 31 minutes

Surface EVAs: 2

EVA time: 7 hours, 45 minutes

*Alan Bean with a tool kit (note Pete Conrad's reflection in his visor).*

After lightning struck Apollo 12 (twice!) during liftoff, it seemed the mission might be aborted. But the rocket kept hurtling toward space—on course! Five days later Pete Conrad and Alan Bean made a pinpoint landing in a group of craters called the Snowman—about 500 feet (152 meters) from Surveyor 3, an unmanned spacecraft that arrived on the moon in 1967. Soon after landing, Alan hammered a long tube into the surface to collect the soil below. Alan and Pete removed Surveyor 3's camera and its robotic metal scoop. They brought this equipment home so scientists could study the effects of the moon's hot days and cold nights on the gear. The Surveyor 3 camera is now on display at the Smithsonian National Air and Space Museum in Washington, DC.

# APOLLO 13

Commander: James "Jim" Lovell Jr. (left)

Command module pilot: John Swigert Jr. (center)

Lunar module pilot: Fred Haise Jr. (right)

Launch: April 11, 1970

Moon landing: None

Splashdown: April 17, 1970

Command module: Odyssey

Lunar module: Aquarius

*The crew of Apollo 13 returns home after an explosion damaged their ship.*

The first two days of Apollo 13's flight went so smoothly that mission control informed the crew, "We're bored to tears down here." On day three the smiling astronauts conducted a live TV broadcast as they hurtled toward the moon. But nine minutes later, everything changed when an oxygen tank exploded. The crew had to figure out how to conserve power, water, and food while ground teams worked to find a way to remove the dangerous carbon dioxide gas building up in the spacecraft. During their harrowing flight, the astronauts lost a total of 31 pounds (14 kilograms) while enduring dehydration and near-freezing temperatures. Fortunately the astronauts made it safely home six days after leaving Earth.

# APOLLO 14

Commander: Alan Shepard Jr. (center)

Command module pilot:
    Stuart "Stu" Roosa (left)

Lunar module pilot:
    Edgar "Ed" Mitchell (right)

Launch: January 31, 1971

Moon landing: February 5, 1971

Splashdown: February 9, 1971

Command module: Kitty Hawk

Lunar module: Antares

Total time on moon: 33 hours, 31 minutes

Surface EVAs: 2

EVA time: 9 hours, 23 minutes

*Alan Shepard with the Modular Equipment Transporter (MET) cart, which carried tools, cameras, and bags for rock samples.*

In May 1961 Alan Shepard became America's first astronaut in space during his short flight in the Freedom 7 capsule. Though he couldn't wait to fly again, a problem in his ears began making him dizzy, and NASA grounded him. After surgery corrected the problem, Alan was chosen for Apollo 14. This mission achieved many goals, such as studying future landing sites and conducting communication and gravity tests. But viewers back home especially enjoyed Alan's golf outing. His first swing buried the ball in moondust. His second and third attempts pushed the ball only a few feet. When Alan's fourth swing finally sent the ball flying, he shouted, "Miles and miles and miles!"

# Apollo 15

Commander: David "Dave" Scott (center)

Command module pilot:
    Alfred "Al" Worden (right)

Lunar module pilot: James "Jim" Irwin (left)

Launch: July 26, 1971

Moon landing: July 30, 1971

Splashdown: August 7, 1971

Command module: Endeavour

Lunar module: Falcon

Total time on moon: 66 hours, 55 minutes

Surface EVAs: 3

EVA time: 18 hours, 35 minutes

*Jim Irwin salutes the flag planted next to Apollo 15's lunar module, Falcon.*

Using the first rover on the moon, the Apollo 15 crew traveled more than three times farther than all earlier missions combined: 17.5 miles (28 kilometers). The men also wore new suits with improved mobility, which allowed them to bend and sit comfortably in the rover. On the second day Dave Scott and Jim Irwin drove to Spur Crater (a large crater about the size of a football field) to hunt for anorthosite rocks. Scientists later determined the white anorthosite rock they brought home was about 4 billion years old. This "Genesis Rock" helped scientists study how the moon formed.

# APOLLO 16

Commander: John Young (center)

Command module pilot:
    Thomas "Ken" Mattingly II (left)

Lunar module pilot:
    Charles "Charlie" Duke Jr. (right)

Launch: April 16, 1972

Moon landing: April 21, 1972

Splashdown: April 27, 1972

Command module: Casper

Lunar module: Orion

Total time on moon: 71 hours, 2 minutes

Surface EVAs: 3

EVA time: 20 hours, 14 minutes

*The Duke family photo included Charlie, his wife, and their two sons.*

Apollo 16 lifted off with a big goal: to prove that the moon isn't geologically "dead." To accomplish this, the astronauts needed to find volcanic rocks, which would show that the moon's inner core is alive with heat. NASA sent them to the Descartes Highlands because scientists believed the craters there had been created by volcanoes. But instead, the crew found rocks created by the impact and heat of meteors smashing into the moon. On the astronauts' third and final EVA, Charlie Duke left a photo of his family for future visitors to find.

# Apollo 17

Commander:
  Eugene "Gene" Cernan (seated)
Command module pilot:
  Ronald "Ron" Evans (right)
Lunar module pilot:
  Harrison "Jack" Schmitt (left)
Launch: December 7, 1972
Moon landing: December 11, 1972
Splashdown: December 19, 1972
Command module: America
Lunar module: Challenger
Total time on moon: 75 hours
Surface EVAs: 3
EVA time: 22 hours, 4 minutes

*Apollo 17 astronauts took this magnificent photo of Earth on their way to the moon.*

The Apollo 17 crew knew they would be the last moon explorers for many years, so they wanted to make the most of their trip. Gene Cernan and Jack Schmitt worked for three exhausting days, collecting more rocks, exploring more area, and taking more photos than any other mission. Like the moon visitors before them, they marveled at the sight of the brilliant blue Earth surrounded by black space. Moved by this incredible view, Gene shared a few words he hoped would unite people from every nation. From his vantage point, it was easy to see that we're all neighbors who share one beautiful planet.

# FOR FURTHER READING

Burleigh, Robert. *One Giant Leap*. New York: Puffin, 2014.

Floca, Brian. *Moonshot: The Flight of Apollo 11*. New York: Atheneum, 2009.

McNulty, Faith. *If You Decide to Go to the Moon*. New York: Scholastic, 2005.

McReynolds, Linda. *Eight Days Gone*. Watertown, MA: Charlesbridge, 2012.

# SOURCE NOTES

Page 7: "That's one small step . . . mankind": Neil Armstrong quoted in "Apollo 11," https://history.nasa.gov/SP-4029/Apollo_11a_Summary.htm.

Page 11: "Good landing, Pete!": Alan Bean quoted in NASA, *Apollo 12 Lunar Surface Journal*, "A Visit to the Snowman," https://www.hq.nasa.gov/alsj/a12/a12.landing.html.

Page 16: "Come on, radar!" [comma and exclamation point added]: Ed Mitchell quoted in NASA, *Apollo 14 Lunar Surface Journal*, "Landing at Fra Mauro," https://www.hq.nasa.gov/alsj/a14/a14.landing.html.

Page 22: "I think we found what we came for!" [exclamation point added]: Dave Scott quoted in NASA, *Apollo 15 Lunar Surface Journal*, "The Genesis Rock," https://www.hq.nasa.gov/alsj/a15/a15.spur.html.

Page 25: "It's just like driving on snow!" [exclamation point added]: John Young quoted in NASA, *Apollo 16 Lunar Surface Journal*, "Grand Prix," https://www.hq.nasa.gov/alsj/a16/a16.trvlm1.html.

Page 29: "We hope . . . peace and harmony": Gene Cernan quoted in NASA, *Apollo 17 Lunar Surface Journal*, "EVA-3 Close-Out," https://www.hq.nasa.gov/alsj/a17/a17.clsout3.html.

Page 41: "We're bored to tears down here": Joe Kerwin, capsule communicator at mission control, quoted in NASA, "Apollo 13: 'Houston, We've Had a Problem . . . ,'" July 8, 2009, https://www.nasa.gov/mission_pages/apollo/missions/apollo13.html.

Page 42: "Miles and miles and miles!" [exclamation point added]: Alan Shepard quoted in NASA, *Apollo 14 Lunar Surface Journal*, "EVA-2 Closeout and the Golf Shots." https://www.hq.nasa.gov/alsj/a14/a14.clsout2.html.

# Selected Bibliography

Aldrin, Buzz, and Malcolm McConnell. *Men from Earth.* New York: Bantam, 1989.

Cernan, Eugene, with Don Davis. *The Last Man on the Moon: Astronaut Eugene Cernan and America's Race in Space.* New York: St. Martin's, 1999.

Chaikin, Andrew. *A Man on the Moon: The Voyages of the Apollo Astronauts.* New York: Viking, 1994.

Lunar and Planetary Institute. "Apollo Missions." http://www.lpi.usra.edu/lunar/missions/apollo/.

NASA. *Apollo Lunar Surface Journal.* Edited by Eric M. Jones and Ken Glover. Last modified December 1, 2017. https://www.hq.nasa.gov/alsj/.

———. "What Was the Saturn V?" September 17, 2010. https://www.nasa.gov/audience/forstudents/5-8/features/nasa-knows/what-was-the-saturn-v-58.html.

NASA History Division. *Apollo Flight Journal.* Edited by David Woods. Last modified February 10, 2017. https://history.nasa.gov/afj/.

———. "The Apollo Program." https://www.hq.nasa.gov/office/pao/History/apollo.html.

Nelson, Craig. *Rocket Men: The Epic Story of the First Men on the Moon.* New York: Viking, 2009.

Reynolds, David West. *Apollo: The Epic Journey to the Moon.* New York: Harcourt, 2002.

Schmitt, Harrison H. "A Field Trip to the Moon." In *NEEP602 Course Notes (Fall 1996): Resources from Space.* University of Wisconsin–Madison, Fusion Technology Institute. Last modified January 24, 2013. http://fti.neep.wisc.edu/neep602/LEC1/trip.htm.

Smithsonian National Air and Space Museum. "The Apollo Program." https://airandspace.si.edu/explore-and-learn/topics/apollo/apollo-program/.

The URLs listed here were accurate at publication, but websites often change. If a URL doesn't work, you can use the internet to find more information.

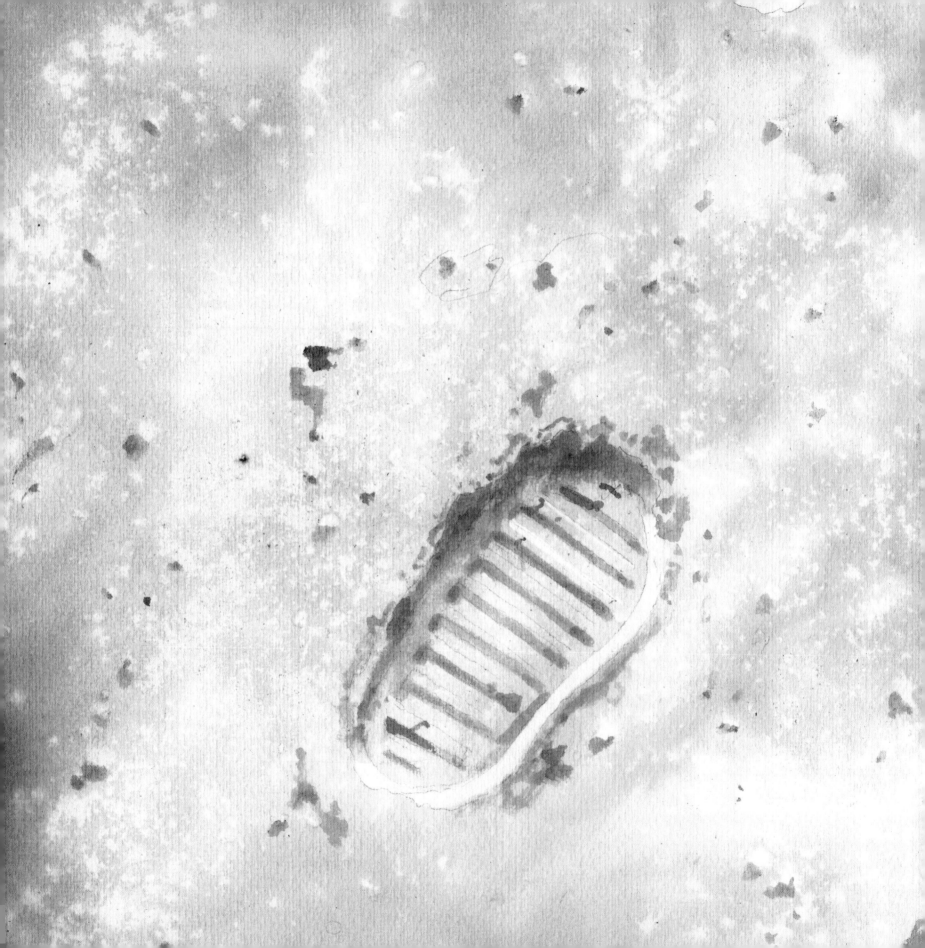

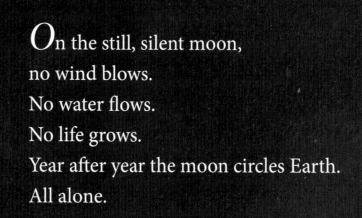

*O*n the still, silent moon,
no wind blows.
No water flows.
No life grows.
Year after year the moon circles Earth.
All alone.

2

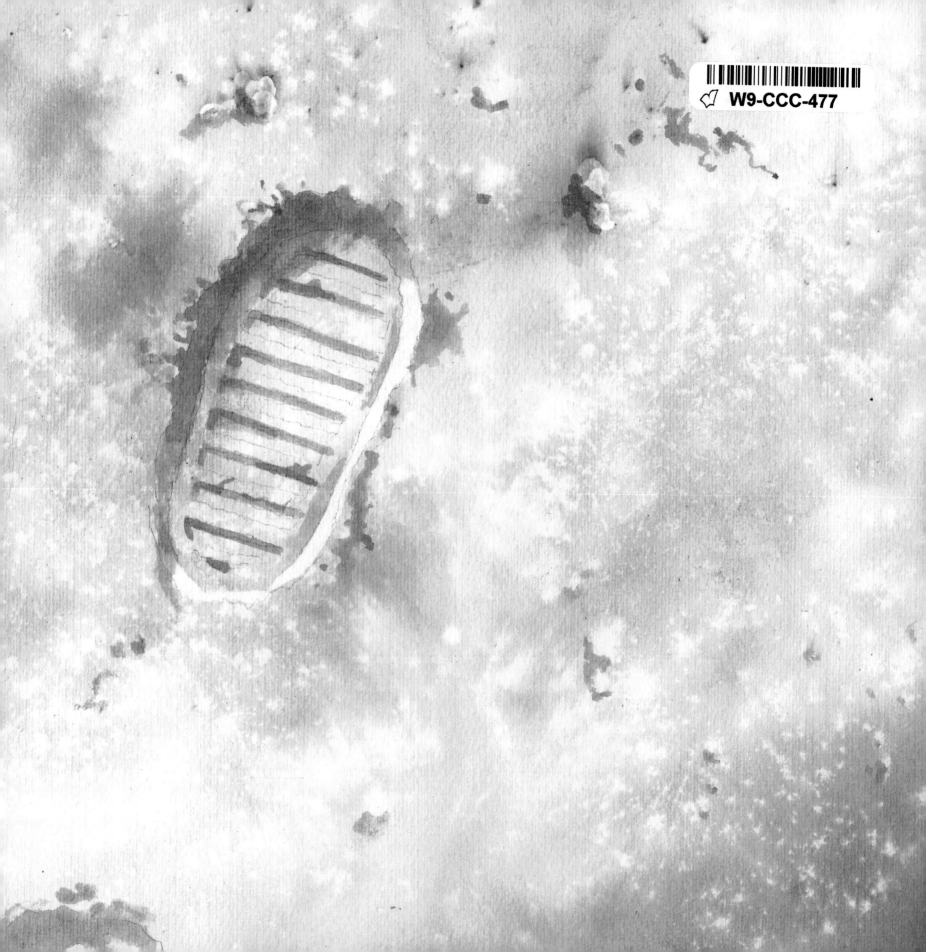